Wean Your Baby with Thermomix®

Wean Your Baby with Thermomix®   1
FIRST FOOD   3
CREAM OF VEGETABLES   4
VEGETABLE PURÉE   5
LETTUCE PURÉE   6
GREEN BEAN PURÉE   7
CORN AND TAPIOCA PURÉE   8
PURÉED CHICKEN   9
BEEF PURÉE   10
CREAM OF HAM   11
PURÉED VEGETABLES   12
SEMOLINA AND CHICKEN   13
CARROT AND CELERY PURÉE   14
APPLE AND BANANA PURÉE   15
PEAR AND APPLE DESSERT   16
BANANA DESSERT   17
APPLE DESSERT   18
GRATED APPLE   19
APPLE AND PEAR DESSERT   20
PEAR AND BANANA DESSERT   21
BANANA WITH LEMON   22
8 MONTHS   23
VEGETABLE BROTH   24
MEAT BROTH   25
PLAICE SOUP   26
SOLE PURÉE   27
HAKE PURÉE   28
FENNEL PURÉE   29
SPINACH PURÉE   31
CREAM OF RICE WITH TOMATO   32
HAKE WITH POTATO   33
SEMOLINA IN BROTH   34
RICE SEMOLINA IN BROTH   35
CORNFLOUR PURÉE   36

SEMOLINA WITH EGG 37
RICE SEMOLINA 38
COOKED BREAD 39
CARROTS IN MILK 40
GREEDY COMPOTE 41
ORANGEY BANANA 42
YOGHURT COMPOTE 43
YOGHURT SMOOTHIE 44
YOGHURT WITH APRICOT 45
FRUIT SNACK 46
YOGHURT WITH CARROTS 47
10 MONTHS 48
PASTINA WITH MILK 48
TURKEY PURÉE 49
ZUCCHINI PURÉE 50
SPINACH PIE 51
SQUASH VELOUTÉ 52
GREEN BEAN VELOUTÉ 53
PURÉED PEACH 54
CORN FLAKE SMOOTHIE 55
CORN FLAKE COMPOTE 56
YOGHURT WITH PINEAPPLE 57
FRESHLY SQUEEZED GRAPEFRUIT 58
SPONGE CAKE 59
GLUTEN-FREE SPONGE CAKE 61
CUSTARD FILLING 62
WHIPPED CREAM 63
SNOW 64
CHOCOLATE SNOW 65
BUTTERCREAM 66
12 MONTHS 67
SWEET PURÉE 67
STEAMED HAKE 68
STEAMED POTATOES 69
STEAMED CARROTS 70
TOMATO VELOUTÉ 71
GRUYERE SOUFFLÉ 72
CARROT SOUFFLÉ 73

MEAT PIE	74
POTATO PIE	75
FISH GRATIN	76
SOLE WITH TOMATO	77
VEGETABLE TART	78
HAM SAUCE	79
HAMBURGER WITH CHEESE	80
HAM WITH SPINACH	81
STEAMED RICE	82
VEGETABLE SOUP	83
SCENTED TOMATO	84
TOMATO SAUCE	85
MILK AND RUSKS	86
COOKIE SMOOTHIE	87
BANANA SMOOTHIE	88
RASPBERRY SMOOTHIE	89
BANANA WITH VANILLA	90
ORANGE DRINK	91
ENGLISH PORRIDGE	92
FIRST ENGLISH BREAKFAST	93
SMOOTHIE WITH RICE FLAKES	94
FRUIT JUICE	95
24 MONTHS	96
FRESH PASTA SHAPES FOR BROTH	96
PEA VELOUTÉ	97
BAKED CELERY	98
SPINACH TART	99
STUFFED, BAKED ARTICHOKES	100
RAW SOUP	101
BOLOGNESE SAUCE	102
STRAWBERRY CAKE	103
STRAWBERRY SNACK	104
COOKIE CAKE	105
CREME ANGLAISE	106
APPLE CAKE	107
APPLE JAM	109
YELLOW MILK	110
CHOCOLATE DRINK	111

PINEAPPLE ICE CREAM 112
EGG WHITE CAKE 113
MIXED FRUIT SORBET 114
RING-SHAPED CAKE 115
DAISY CAKE 117
WHOLEMEAL DRINK 119
SHORTCRUST PASTRY COOKIES 120
PRECOOKED RICE FLOUR 121
GLUTEN-FREE PASTA SHAPES FOR BROTH 122
DOUGH FOR GLUTEN-FREE BREAD 123
DOUGH FOR GLUTEN-FREE PASTA 124
GLUTEN-FREE APPLE CAKE 124
GLUTEN-FREE CAMILLE 126
GREEN APPLE MOUSSE 127
FRUIT JELLO 128

6 months: the adventure begins!

FIRST FOOD

Ingredients:

- 50 g / 1.8 oz peeled potatoes
- 50 g / 1.8 oz carrots
- 40 g / 1.4 oz veal
- 20 g / 0.7 oz instant cream of rice
- 250 g / 8.8 oz water
- 1 teaspoon extra virgin olive oil

Method:

1. With the blade in motion, insert the meat and vegetables through the hole in the lid.

2. Add the water and cook for 12 minutes at 90°-100° C / 195°-210° F, speed 2

3. When cooked, combine with the cream of rice and mix together for 40 seconds, speed 6

4. Pour out the purée and add a teaspoon of oil.

CREAM OF VEGETABLES

Ingredients:

- 50 g / 1.8 oz peeled potatoes
- 50 g / 1.8 oz carrots
- 3 lettuce leaves
- 40 g / 1.4 oz chicken breast
- 20 g / 0.7 oz instant cream of rice
- 250 g / 8.8 oz water
- 1 teaspoon extra virgin olive oil

Method:

1. With the blade in motion (speed 7), insert the chopped meat and vegetables through the hole in the lid

2. Add the water and cook for 12 minutes at 90°-100° C / 195°-210° F, speed 2

3. When cooked, combine with the cream of rice and mix together for 40 seconds at speed 6

VEGETABLE PURÉE

Ingredients:

- 30 g / 1.1 oz peeled potatoes
- 30 g / 1.1 oz carrots
- 30 g / 1.1 oz zucchini
- 2 lettuce leaves
- 1 small piece celery
- 40 g / 1.4 oz chicken
- 20 g / 0.7 oz instant cream of rice
- 250 g / 8.8 oz water
- 1 teaspoon extra virgin olive oil

Method:

1. With the blade in motion (speed 7), insert the chicken, lettuce, potatoes, zucchini, carrots and celery through the hole in the lid

2. Add the water and cook for 12 minutes at 90°-100° C / 195°-210° F, speed 2

3. When cooked, combine with the cream of rice and mix together for 40 seconds, speed 6

4. Pour out the purée and add a teaspoon of oil.

LETTUCE PURÉE

Ingredients:

- 100 g / 3.5 oz potatoes
- 40 g / 1.4 oz veal
- 20 g / 0.7 oz instant semolina
- 2 lettuce leaves (about 30 g)
- 250 g / 8.8 oz water
- 1 teaspoon extra virgin olive oil

Method:

1. With the blade in motion (speed 7), insert the chopped meat and vegetables through the hole in the lid.

2. Add the water and cook for 12 minutes at 90°-100° C / 195°-210° F, speed 2

3. When cooked, combine with the cream of rice and mix together for 40 seconds, speed 6

4. Pour out the purée and add a teaspoon of oil.

GREEN BEAN PURÉE

Ingredients:

- 100 g / 3.5 oz green beans
- 40 g / 1.4 oz rabbit
- 20 g / 0.7 oz pastina (small pasta shapes)
- 250 g / 8.8 oz water
- 1 teaspoon extra virgin olive oil

Method:

1. With the blade in motion (speed 7), insert the meat and beans through the hole in the lid. Add the water and pasta and cook for 12 minutes at 90°-100° C /195°-210° F, speed 2

2. When cooked, combine with the cream of rice and mix together for 40 seconds, speed 6

3. Pour out the purée and add a teaspoon of oil.

CORN AND TAPIOCA PURÉE

Ingredients:

- 100 g / 3.5 oz green beans
- 20 g / 0.7 oz turkey
- 20 g / 0.7 oz instant cream of corn and tapioca
- 200 g / 7 oz milk
- 100 g / 3.5 oz water
- 1 teaspoon extra virgin olive oil

Method:

1. With the blade in motion (speed 7), insert the meat and green beans. Add the water and milk and cook for 12 minutes at 90° C /195° F, speed 2
2. When cooked, add the cream of corn and tapioca through the hole in the lid
3. Blend for 40 seconds, speed 6
4. Pour out the purée and add a teaspoon of oil.

PURÉED CHICKEN

Ingredients:

- 120 g / 7.1 oz vegetable
- 40 g / 1.4 oz chicken
- 20 g / 0.7 oz instant cream of rice
- 250 g / 8.8 oz water
- 1 teaspoon extra virgin olive oil

Method:

1. With the blade in motion (speed 7), insert the meat and vegetables through the hole in the lid.
2. Add the water and cook for 12 minutes at 90°-100° C / 195°-210° F, speed 2
3. When cooked, combine with the cream of rice and mix together for 40 seconds, speed 6
4. Pour out the purée and add a teaspoon of oil.

BEEF PURÉE

Ingredients:

- 50 g / 1.8 oz peeled potatoes
- 50 g / 1.8 oz carrots
- 40 g / 1.4 oz beef
- 20 g / 0.7 oz pastina (small pasta shapes)
- 300 g / 10.6 oz water
- 1 teaspoon extra virgin olive oil

Method:

1. With the blade in motion (speed 7), insert the meat and vegetables
2. Stir the mixture with the spatula, add the water and cook for 15 minutes at 90°-100° C/ 195°-210° F, speed 2
3. Blend for 40 seconds, speed 6
4. Add the pastina and cook for 4 minutes at 90°-100° C/ 195°-210° F, speed 1
5. Pour out the mixture and add a teaspoon of oil.

CREAM OF HAM

Ingredients:

- 120 g / 7 oz peeled potatoes
- 20 g / 0.7 oz lean ham
- 2 lettuce leaves
- 20 g / 0.7 oz instant semolina
- 250 g /8.8 water
- 1 teaspoon extra virgin olive oil

Method:

1. Put the chopped lettuce and potatoes in the mixing bowl. Over 20 seconds, gradually increase the speed from 1 – 8.

2. Add the water and cook for 12 minutes at 90°-100° C/195°-210° F speed 2

3. When cooked, insert the semolina and chopped ham through the hole in the lid and blend for 20 seconds at speed 4 and 15 seconds at speed 8

4. Pour out the mixture and add a teaspoon of oil.

PURÉED VEGETABLES

Ingredients:

- 350 g / 12.3 oz mixed vegetables
- 500 g / 17.6 oz water

Method:

1. Put the vegetables in the mixing bowl. Over 30 seconds, gradually increase the speed from 1 to 8
2. Add the water and cook for 15 minutes at 100° C / 210° F, speed 4

SEMOLINA AND CHICKEN

Ingredients:

- 80 g / 2.8 oz peeled potatoes
- 40 g / 1.4 oz chicken breast
- 2 lettuce leaves
- 20 g / 0.7 oz instant semolina
- 250 g / 8.8 oz water
- 1 teaspoon extra virgin olive oil

Method:

1. With the blade in motion (speed 7), add the chicken and vegetables
2. Add the water and cook for 12 minutes at 90°-100° C /195°-210° F, speed 2
3. When cooked, combine with the cream of rice and mix together for 40 seconds, speed 6
4. Pour out the purée and add a teaspoon of oil.

CARROT AND CELERY PURÉE

Ingredients:

- 150 g / 5.3 oz carrots
- 50 g / 1.8 oz celery hearts
- 50 g / 1.8 oz peeled potatoes
- 40 g / 1.4 oz cooked beef
- 20 g / 0.7 oz instant rice semolina
- 300 g / 10.6 oz water
- 1 teaspoon extra virgin olive oil

Method:

1. Put the vegetables cut into small pieces in the mixing bowl for 10 seconds, speed 3
2. Mix with the spatula. Add the water and cook for 12 minutes at 90°-100° C /195°-210° F, speed 2
3. Blend for 40 seconds, speed 6
4. Remove half the mixture, add the beef and the semolina and blend for 40 seconds, speed 6
5. Pour out the purée and add a teaspoon of oil.

APPLE AND BANANA PURÉE

Ingredients:

- 80 g / 2.8 oz peeled apple
- 40 g / 1.1 oz banana
- 75 g / 2.6 oz water
- a few drops of lemon juice

Method:

1. Put the apple and banana in the mixing bowl for 10 seconds, speed 4
2. Add the water and lemon juice and cook for 5 minutes at 90° C/ 195° F, speed 4
3. When cooked, blend for 20 seconds, speed 6
4. Pour into a cup, cover and leave to cool.

PEAR AND APPLE DESSERT

Ingredients:

- 60 g / 2.1 oz peeled apple
- 60 g / 2.1 oz peeled pear
- 75 g / 2.6 oz water
- a few drops of lemon juice

Method:

1. Put the apple and pear in the mixing bowl for 10 seconds, speed 4
2. Add the water and lemon juice and cook for 5 minutes at 90° C/ 195° F, speed 4
3. When cooked, blend for 20 seconds, speed 6
4. Pour into a cup, cover and leave to cool.

BANANA DESSERT

Ingredients:

- 120 g / 4.2 oz banana
- 75 g / 2.6 oz water
- a few drops of lemon juice

Method:

1. Put the banana in the mixing bowl for 10 seconds, speed 4
2. Add the water and lemon for 40 seconds at speed 6 and 20 seconds at speed 8

APPLE DESSERT

Ingredients:

- 120 g / 4.2 oz peeled apple
- 75 g / 2.6 oz water
- a few drops of lemon juice

Method:

1. Put the apple in the mixing bowl for 10 seconds, speed 4
2. Add the water and lemon juice and cook for 5 minutes at 90° C/195° F, speed 4
3. When cooked, blend for 20 seconds, speed 6
4. Pour into a cup, cover and leave to cool.

GRATED APPLE

Ingredients:

- 120 g / 4.2 oz peeled apple
- 50 g / 1.8 oz water
- 2 teaspoons of lemon juice

Method:

1. With the blade in motion (speed 7), add the chopped apple to the mixing bowl
2. Stir the mixture with the spatula and add the water and lemon juice for 40 seconds, speed 8
3. Serve immediately.

APPLE AND PEAR DESSERT

Ingredients:

- 60 g / 2.1 oz peeled apple
- 60 g / 2.1 oz peeled pear
- 100 g / 3.5 oz water
- 1 teaspoon of lemon juice

Method:

1. With the blade in motion (speed 4), insert the chopped apple and pear through the hole in the lid.
2. Stir the mixture with the spatula and add the water and juice for 40 seconds, speed 9
3. Serve immediately.

PEAR AND BANANA DESSERT

Ingredients:

- 60 g / 2.1 oz peeled apple
- 60 g / 2.1 oz banana
- 100 g / 3.5 oz water
- 1 teaspoon of lemon juice

Method:

1. With the blade in motion (speed 4), insert the chopped banana and pear through the hole in the lid.
2. Stir the mixture with the spatula
3. Add the water and lemon juice for 40 seconds, speed 9
4. Serve immediately.

BANANA WITH LEMON

Ingredients:

- 120 g / 4.2 oz banana
- 70 g / 2.5 oz water
- 1 teaspoon of lemon juice

Method:

1. With the blade in motion (speed 4), insert the chopped banana through the hole in the lid.
2. Stir the mixture with the spatula
3. Add the water and lemon juice for 40 seconds, speed 9
4. Serve immediately while fresh

8 MONTHS

VEGETABLE BROTH

Ingredients:

- 1 medium potato, peeled
- 1 piece of celery
- 1 zucchini
- 2-3 spinach, lettuce or other green leaves
- 500 g / 17.6 oz water

Method:

1. Add the water and the vegetables cut into large chunks to the mixing bowl
2. Cook for 20 minutes at 100° C / 210° F, speed 1
3. Strain and use the broth as the base for different dishes

MEAT BROTH

Ingredients:

- 100 g / 3.5 oz cubed beef or chicken
- 100 g / 3.5 oz mixed vegetables
- 500 g / 17.6 oz water

Method:

1. Put all the ingredients in the mixing bowl and cook for 20 minutes at 90°- 100° C / 195°-210° F, speed 1
2. Strain and use the broth as a base for different dishes.

PLAICE SOUP

Ingredients:

- 150 g / 5.3 oz mixed vegetables
- 50 g / 1.8 oz plaice
- 400 g / 14 oz water
- 20 g / 0.7 oz pastina (small pasta shapes)
- 1 teaspoon extra virgin olive oil

Method:

1. Add the water, fish and roughly chopped vegetables to the mixing bowl for 5 seconds, speed 7
2. Cook for 5 minutes at 90°-100° C /195°-210° F, speed 1
3. Pour out the purée and add a teaspoon of oil.

SOLE PURÉE

Ingredients:

- 100 g / 3.5 oz carrots
- 50 g / 1.8 oz peeled potatoes
- 50 g / 1.8 oz sole fillet
- 20 g / 0.7 oz instant semolina
- 400 g / 14 oz water
- 1 teaspoon extra virgin olive oil

Method:

1. With the blade in motion (speed 6), insert the potatoes, carrots and sole through the hole in the lid.
2. Add the water and cook for 12 minutes at 90°-100° C /195°-210° F, speed 2
3. When cooked, add the semolina through the hole in the lid and blend for 40 seconds, speed 6
4. Pour out the purée and add a teaspoon of oil.

HAKE PURÉE

Ingredients:

- 100 g / 3.5 oz peeled potatoes
- 25 g / 0.9 oz instant cream of rice
- 40 g / 1.4 oz hake
- 400 g / 14 oz water
- 1 sprig parsley
- 1 teaspoon extra virgin olive oil

Method:

1. With the blade in motion (speed 6), insert the potato and fish through the hole in the lid.
2. Add water and cook for 20 minutes at 90°-100° C/195°-210° F, speed 2
3. When cooked, add the cream of rice and parsley through the lid.
4. Blend for 40 seconds, speed 6
5. Pour out the purée and add a teaspoon of oil.

FENNEL PURÉE

Ingredients:

- 200 g / 7 oz fennel
- 100 g / 3.5 oz peeled potatoes
- 40 g / 1.4 oz sole fillets
- 25 g / 0.9 oz pastina (small pasta shapes)
- 400 g / 14 oz water
- 1 sprig parsley
- 1 teaspoon extra virgin olive oil

Method:

1. With the blade in motion (speed 6), add the potato and fennel through the hole in the lid
2. Stir the mixture with the spatula
3. Add water and cook for 10 minutes at 90°-100° C/195°-210° F, speed 2
4. Remove half the mixture and add the sole for 40 seconds, speed 4
5. Add the pasta and cook for 8 minutes at 90° c/195° F, speed 1
6. Pour out the purée and add a teaspoon of oil.

NOTE: The half of the mixture which was removed can be used for the evening meal by adding semolina or cream of rice

SPINACH PURÉE

Ingredients:

- 80 g / 2.8 oz peeled potatoes
- 40 g / 1.4 oz chicken
- A few spinach leaves
- 200 g / 7 oz water
- 25 g / 0.9 oz cornflour
- 1 teaspoon extra virgin olive oil

Method:

1. With the blade in motion (speed 7), add the chopped chicken and potato through the hole in the lid
2. Add water and cook for 10 minutes at 90°-100° C/195°-210° F, speed 2
3. After half the cooking time has passed, add the spinach
4. When cooked, blend for 40 seconds, speed 4
5. Add the cornflour through the hole in the lid and cook for 5 minutes at 90° C/195° F, speed 1
6. Pour out the purée and add a teaspoon of oil.

CREAM OF RICE WITH TOMATO

Ingredients:

- 100 g / 3.5 oz peeled and deseeded tomatoes
- 40 g / 1.4 oz chicken or turkey breast
- 25 g / 0.9 oz rice
- 200 g / 7 oz water
- 1 teaspoon extra virgin olive oil

Method:

1. With the blade in motion (speed 6), add the chicken and tomato through the hole in the lid.
2. Stir the mixture with the spatula
3. Add rice and water for 25 minutes at 90°-100° C/195°-210° F, speed 2
4. When cooked, blend for 10 seconds, speed 6
5. Pour out the purée and add a teaspoon of oil.

HAKE WITH POTATO

Ingredients:

- 100 g / 3.5 oz peeled potatoes
- 40 g / 1.4 oz hake
- 500 g / 17.6 oz water
- 1 teaspoon extra virgin olive oil
- 1 teaspoon grated parmesan

Method:

Put the water and the basket containing the cubed potatoes into the mixing bowl for 20 minutes at 100° C/210° F, speed 1

1. Halfway through the cooking time, add the hake through the hole in the lid
2. When cooked remove the basket, retaining 200 g / 7 oz of cooking water
3. Blend the potato and hake for 40 seconds, speed 6
4. Pour out the purée and add a teaspoon of oil and a teaspoon of parmesan.

SEMOLINA IN BROTH

Ingredients:

- 25 g / 0.9 oz instant semolina
- 200 g / 7 oz meat broth
- 2 teaspoons tomato purée
- 1 teaspoon extra virgin olive oil

Method:

1. Put the broth and tomato into the mixing bowl for 5 minutes and 90°-100° C/195°-210° F, speed 1
2. Add the semolina through the hole in the lid and blend for 40 seconds, speed 6
3. Pour out the purée and add a teaspoon of oil.

RICE SEMOLINA IN BROTH

Ingredients:

- 25 g / 0.9 oz instant rice semolina
- 200 g / 7 oz vegetable broth
- 80 g / 2.8 oz cooked greens
- 1 teaspoon extra virgin olive oil

Method:

1. Put the broth into the mixing bowl for 5 minutes at 90°-100° C/195°-210° F, speed 1
2. Add the vegetables and semolina through the hole in the lid and blend for 40 seconds, speed 6
3. Pour out the purée and add a teaspoon of oil.

CORNFLOUR PURÉE

Ingredients:

- 25 g / 0.9 oz cornflour
- 200 g / 7 oz meat broth
- 1 teaspoon extra virgin olive oil

Method:

1. Add the broth and cornflour to the mixing bowl and cook for 8 minutes at 80° C/ 175° F, speed 3
2. Pour out the purée and add a teaspoon of oil.

SEMOLINA WITH EGG

Ingredients:

- 25 g / 0.9 oz instant semolina
- 200 g / 7 oz meat or vegetable broth
- 1 hardboiled egg yolk
- 1 teaspoon extra virgin olive oil

Method:

1. Put the broth into the mixing bowl and cook for 5 minutes at 90°-100° C/195°-210° F, speed 1
2. Add the semolina and egg yolk through the hole in the lid
3. Blend for 40 seconds, speed 6
4. Pour out the purée and add a teaspoon of oil.

RICE SEMOLINA

Ingredients:

- 25 g / 0.9 oz instant semolina rice
- 200 g / 7 oz chicken broth

Method:

1. Put the broth in the mixing bowl
2. Cook for 5 minutes at 90°-100° C/195°-210° F, speed 1
3. Add the semolina through the lid
4. Blend for 40 seconds, speed 6
5. Pour out the purée

COOKED BREAD

Ingredients:

- 30 g / 1.1 oz bread
- 200 g / 7 oz broth
- 1 teaspoon grated parmesan
- 1 teaspoon extra virgin olive oil

Method:

1. Put the bread in the mixing bowl for 20 seconds, speed 3
2. Add the broth and cook for 5 minutes at 80° C/175° F, speed 2
3. Pour into a dish and add the oil and parmesan

CARROTS IN MILK

Ingredients:

- 80 g / 2.8 oz carrots
- 200 g / 7 oz milk
- 15 g / 0.5 oz cornflour

Method:

1. Put carrots into the mixing bowl for 10 seconds, speed 9
2. Add the milk and cook for 15 minutes at 90° C/195° F, speed 2
3. When cooked, add the cornflour with the blade in motion
4. Cook for 5 minutes at 90° C/195° F, speed 3

GREEDY COMPOTE

Ingredients:

- 60 g / 2.1 oz banana
- 60 g / 2.1 oz apricot
- 50 g / 1.8 oz water
- 1 teaspoon lemon juice

Method:

1. With the blade in motion (speed 4), add the chopped fruit to the mixing bowl
2. Stir the mixture with the spatula. Add the water and juice for 40 seconds, speed 9
3. Serve immediately.

ORANGEY BANANA

Ingredients:

- 100 g / 3.5 oz banana
- 1\2 measuring cup orange juice
- 50 g / 1.8 oz water

Method:

1. With the blade in motion (speed 4), add the chopped fruit to the mixing bowl
2. Stir the mixture with the spatula
3. Add the water and juice for 40 seconds, speed 9
4. Serve immediately.

YOGHURT COMPOTE

Ingredients:

- 2 cookies
- 1\2 peeled fruit
- 1 pot of natural yoghurt (125g)

Method:

1. With the blade in motion (speed 4), add the cookies to the mixing bowl
2. Crush for 30 seconds, speed 6
3. With the blade in motion, add the fruit
4. Stir the mixture with the spatula and add the yoghurt for 5 seconds, speed 2
5. Serve immediately.

YOGHURT SMOOTHIE

Ingredients:

- 1 rusk
- 50 g / 1.8 oz banana
- 1 pot natural yoghurt (125 g/ 4.4 oz)

Method:

1. With the blade in motion (speed 4), add the banana to the mixing bowl
2. Stir the mixture with the spatula
3. Add the yoghurt for 30 seconds, speed 5
4. Serve immediately

YOGHURT WITH APRICOT

Ingredients:

- 50 g / 1.8 oz ripe apricot
- 1 pot of natural yoghurt
- 1 teaspoon of sugar (recommended)

Method:

1. With the blade in motion (speed 4), add the apricot to the mixing bowl
2. Stir the mixture with the spatula
3. Add yoghurt and sugar for 5 seconds, speed 2
4. Serve immediately.

FRUIT SNACK

Ingredients:

- 1 orange
- 80 g / 2.8 oz banana
- 80 g / 2.8 oz apple
- 1 teaspoon of sugar

Method:

1. Chop the orange and remove the seeds. Put in the mixing bowl for 20 seconds, speed 6
2. Add the chopped apple and banana for 40 seconds, speed 6
3. Stir the mixture with the spatula and blend with the sugar for 20 seconds, speed 8
4. Serve immediately.

YOGHURT WITH CARROTS

Ingredients:

- 50 g / 1.8 oz apple
- 20 g / 0.7 oz carrot
- 1 pot of natural yoghurt

Method:

1. With the blade in motion (speed 4), add the apple and carrot
2. Stir the mixture with the spatula
3. Add the yoghurt for 10 seconds, speed 4
4. Serve immediately.

10 MONTHS

PASTINA WITH MILK

Ingredients:

- 30 g / 1.1 oz pastina (small pasta shapes)
- 50 g / 1.8 oz water
- 100 g / 3.5 oz milk

Method:

1. Place the water, milk and pastina in the mixing bowl
2. Cook for 10 minutes at 90° C/195° F, speed 1
3. Pour out the mixture and let it cool down.

TURKEY PURÉE

Ingredients:

- 40 g / 1.4 oz carrots
- 40 g / 1.4 oz peeled potatoes
- 40 g / 1.4 oz turkey
- 150 g / 5.3 oz milk
- 50 g / 1.8 oz water
- 1 teaspoon extra virgin olive oil

Method:

1. With the blade in motion (speed 7) add the turkey through the hole in the lid
2. Add the vegetables for 20 seconds, speed 3
3. Stir the mixture with the spatula
4. Add the water and milk and cook for 13 minutes at 90° C/195° F, speed 2
5. When cooked, blend for 40 seconds, speed 6
6. Pour out the purée and add a teaspoon of oil.

ZUCCHINI PURÉE

Ingredients:

- 100 g / 3.5 oz zucchini
- 80 g / 2.8 oz peeled potatoes
- 200 g / 7 oz water
- 20 g / 0.7 oz grated parmesan
- 1 egg yolk
- 1 teaspoon extra virgin olive oil

Method:

1. Add the zucchini, potato and water and cook for 15 minutes at 90°-100° C/195°-210° F, speed 1
2. Add the parmesan and egg yolk for 2 minutes at 80° C/175° F, speed 2
3. Pour out the purée and add a teaspoon of oil.

SPINACH PIE

Ingredients:

- 100 g / 3.5 oz washed spinach
- 100 g / 3.5 oz peeled potatoes
- 400 g / 14 oz water
- 30 g / 1.1 oz grated parmesan
- 50 g / 1.8 oz milk
- 1 teaspoon extra virgin olive oil

Method:

1. Add first the spinach, then the cubed potatoes to the mixing bowl for 10 seconds, speed 6
2. Add the water and milk and cook for 10 minutes at 90°-100° C/195°-210° F, speed 2
3. Add the parmesan and oil and pour the mixture into a small baking tray
4. Cook in a preheated oven at 180° C/360° F for about 15 minutes.
5. Serve warm.

SQUASH VELOUTÉ

Ingredients:

- 100 g / 3.5 oz squash
- 70 g / 2.5 oz peeled potatoes
- 150 g / 5.3 oz milk
- 100 g / 3.5 oz water
- 1 teaspoon extra virgin olive oil

Method:

1. Place the cubed squash and potato in the mixing bowl for 20 seconds, speed 5
2. Stir the mixture with the spatula. Add the water and milk and cook for 15 minutes at 90° C/185° F, speed 2
3. When cooked, blend for 40 seconds, speed 6
4. Pour out the velouté and add a teaspoon of oil.

Note: If you wish, you can add 10 g / 0.4 oz of parmesan

GREEN BEAN VELOUTÉ

Ingredients:

- 100 g / 3.5 oz green beans
- 300 g / 10.6 oz water
- 200 g / 7 oz milk
- 2 teaspoons of starch
- 10 g / 0.4 oz grated parmesan

Method:

1. Position the butterfly whisk
2. Add the green beans and water and cook for 20 minutes at 100° C/210° F, speed 1
3. Remove the cooking water and butterfly whisk
4. Add the parmesan for 20 seconds, speed 6
5. Mix in the milk and starch for 25 seconds, speed 9
6. Cook for 7 minutes at 90° C/195° F, speed 2
7. When cooked, blend for 40 seconds, speed 6

PURÉED PEACH

Ingredients:

- 120 g / 4.2 oz peeled peach
- 50 g / 1.8 oz water
- 1 teaspoon of lemon juice

Method:

1. With the blade in motion (speed 4), add the peach through the hole in the lid
2. Add the water and juice
3. Cook for 3 minutes at 90° C/195° F, speed 2
4. Stir the mixture with the spatula
5. Blend for 40 seconds, speed 6
6. Serve cold

CORN FLAKE SMOOTHIE

Ingredients:

- 20 g / 0.7 oz cornflakes
- 2 flat tablespoons of jam
- 1 pot of natural yoghurt (125 g / 4.4 oz)

Method:

1. Crush the cornflakes for 50 seconds, turbo speed
2. Add the other ingredients for 10 seconds, speed 3
3. Stir the mixture with the spatula and blend for 5 seconds, speed 2.

CORN FLAKE COMPOTE

Ingredients:

- 50 g / 1.8 oz peeled apple
- 20 g / 0.7 oz Corn Flakes
- 1 pot of natural yoghurt (125 g / 4.4 oz)

Method:

1. Crush the cornflakes for 50 seconds, turbo speed
2. With the blade in motion (speed 4 for 10 seconds), add the apple through the hole in the lid.
3. Stir the mixture with the spatula and add the yoghurt for 30 seconds, speed 4.

Note: If you wish you can add 1 teaspoon of honey

YOGHURT WITH PINEAPPLE

Ingredients:

- 1 slice fresh pineapple
- 1 pot of natural yoghurt (125 g / 4.4 oz)
- 50 g / 1.8 oz milk
- 1 teaspoon of sugar

Method:

1. Remove the core from the pineapple slice and chop into pieces
2. With the blade in motion (speed 4), add the pineapple through the hole in the lid
3. Stir the mixture with the spatula and add the milk and sugar for 30 seconds, speed 8
4. Add the yoghurt for 5 seconds, speed 2

FRESHLY SQUEEZED GRAPEFRUIT

Ingredients:

- Pulp of half a grapefruit
- 50 g / 1.8 oz water
- 1 teaspoon of sugar

Method:

1. Put all ingredients in the mixing bowl for 40 seconds, speed 6
2. Strain and serve

Note: the grapefruit can be substituted with orange

First Birthday

SPONGE CAKE

Ingredients:

- 250 g / 8.8 oz flour
- 250 g / 8.8 oz sugar
- 6 eggs
- 1 sachet dried yeast
- a pinch of salt

Method:

1. Put the sugar in the mixing bowl for 10 seconds at turbo speed
2. Add the eggs for 20 seconds, speed 4
3. With the blade in motion (speed 3), add the flour through the hole and mix for 5 minutes
4. Add the yeast for 30 seconds, speed 3
5. Pour the mixture into a greased and floured baking tray (25 cm / 10 in diameter and 4 cm /1 ½ in high)

6. Cook in a preheated oven at 160° C / 320° F for 10 minutes, then at 180° C/ 360° F for 15 minutes and at 200° C/390° F for a final 15 minutes

7. Switch off the oven and leave it to rest there for a few minutes before serving.

GLUTEN-FREE SPONGE CAKE

Ingredients:

- 3 measuring cups gluten-free flour
- 200 g / 7 oz sugar
- 6 eggs
- 1 sachet of gluten-free baking powder
- 1 sachet vanilla flavoring
- A pinch of salt

Method:

1. Position the butterfly whisk and introduce the sugar, salt and eggs for 6 minutes, speed 3
2. Without stopping the machine, add the flour one measuring cup at a time, with the vanilla and baking powder. Mix for 8 minutes, speed 3
3. Pour the mixture into a greased and floured cake tin
4. Cook in a preheated oven at 160° C/ 320° F for 15 minutes then 180° C /360° F for 20 minutes
5. Switch off the oven and leave it to rest there for a few minutes before serving.

CUSTARD FILLING

Ingredients:

- 500 g / 17.6 oz milk
- 2 eggs and 1 yolk
- 100 g / 3.5 oz sugar
- 40 g / 1.4 oz flour or cornflour
- Lemon zest or vanilla flavoring

Method:

1. Put all the ingredients in the mixing bowl for 5 seconds, speed 4
2. Cook for 7 minutes at 80° C/175° F, speed 2
3. Leave to cool.

Orange version: add the juice of 2 oranges

Chocolate version: when cooked add 100 g/ 3.5 oz dark chocolate

Chantilly version: add 200 g / 7 oz whipped cream to the cold custard

WHIPPED CREAM

Ingredients:

- 400 g / 14 oz fresh cream or non-dairy cream

Method:

1. Position the butterfly whisk and add the chilled cream for 50 seconds, speed 3

Note: If you want to sweeten the cream, add icing sugar before whisking.

- *Chocolate version*: add 1\2 measure of bitter cocoa powder to the cream
- *Coffee version:* add a tablespoon of instant coffee granules

Decorations

SNOW

Ingredients:

- 200 g/ 7 oz sugar
- 1 egg white
- 1 teaspoon of lemon juice

Method:

1. Make sure the mixing bowl is completely dry, then add the sugar for 30 seconds at turbo speed until you obtain a fine powder.
2. Add the egg white and the lemon juice for 30 seconds, speed 4

CHOCOLATE SNOW

Ingredients:

- 100 g / 3.5 oz dark chocolate
- 200 g / 7 oz sugar
- 100 g / 3.5 oz water
- 30 g / 1.1 oz butter

Method:

1. Make sure the mixing bowl is completely dry, then add the sugar for 30 seconds at turbo speed until you obtain a fine powder.
2. Remove the sugar and place in a bowl
3. With the blade in motion (speed 6) add the chopped chocolate through the hole in the lid
4. Add the water and sugar for 5 minutes at 70° C/160° F, speed 1
5. Leave to cool then add the butter for 10 seconds, speed 2

BUTTERCREAM

Ingredients:

- 100 g / 3.5 oz butter
- 50 g / 1.8 oz icing sugar

Method:

- Position the butterfly whisk and add all the ingredients for 15 seconds, speed 2

Note: If you wish, you can dye the buttercream with food coloring.

12 MONTHS

SWEET PURÉE

Ingredients:

- 20 g / 0.7 oz instant semolina
- 200 g / 7 oz milk
- 100 g / 3.5 oz water
- 1 teaspoon of sugar

Method:

1. Put the milk, water and sugar in the mixing bowl for 4 minutes at 90° C/195° F, speed 2
2. With the blade in motion, add the semolina through the hole in the lid for 30 seconds, speed 3
3. Pour out the purée and leave to cool.

STEAMED HAKE

Ingredients:

- 70 g / 2.5 oz hake
- 300 g / 10.6 oz water
- 1 teaspoon of lemon juice
- 1 teaspoon of extra virgin olive oil
- a pinch of salt

Method:

1. Add the water and put the chopped hake in the basket
2. Cook for 12 minutes at 100° C/210° F, speed 1
3. When cooked, serve the hake with oil and lemon.

Note: You can substitute the hake with sole, cod or trout.

STEAMED POTATOES

Ingredients:

- Potatoes

Method:

1. Add water to the mixing bowl and place the cubed potatoes in the basket
2. Cook for 20 minutes at 100° C/210° F, speed 4
3. When cooked, remove the potatoes from the basket.

Depending on the age of the child the potato can be served with oil, or blended for 20 seconds at speed 6ì with half a measure of water, then dressed with oil.

STEAMED CARROTS

Ingredients:

- carrots (amount adjusted to the age of the child)
- 500 g / 17.6 oz water
- 1 teaspoon extra virgin olive oil
- a pinch of salt.

Method:

1. Put the water in the mixing bowl and the chopped carrots into the basket
2. Cook for 25 minutes at 100° C/210° F, speed 4

When cooked, remove the carrots from the basket. Depending on the age of the child, serve dressed with oil, or place the carrots in the mixing bowl and blend for 20 seconds, speed 6. If necessary add half a measure of water and dress with oil.

TOMATO VELOUTÉ

Ingredients:

- 50 g / 1.8 oz cooked potato
- 1 ripe tomato
- 100 g / 3.5 oz water
- 50 g / 1.8 oz milk
- 1 teaspoon extra virgin olive oil
- a pinch of salt

Method:

1. Put the tomato, water and salt into the mixing bowl for 20 seconds, speed 5
2. Cook for 10 minutes at 90° C/195° F, speed 2
3. Add the cubed potato and milk and mix for 40 seconds, speed 6
4. Pour out the velouté and add a a teaspoon of oil

GRUYERE SOUFFLÉ

Ingredients:

- 30 g / 1.1 oz gruyere
- 1 egg
- 50 g / 1.8 oz milk
- 50 g / 1.8 oz potato starch
- 1 knob of butter

Method:

1. With the blade in motion, put the in the mixing bowl at speed 4 for 30 seconds
2. Add the other ingredients for 30 seconds, speed 6
3. Stir the mixture with the spatula and blend for 30 seconds, speed 9
4. Pour the mixture into a small buttered tin (18 cm /7 in diameter)
5. Cook in a preheated oven at 150° C/300° F for about 10 minutes.

CARROT SOUFFLÉ

Ingredients:

- 100 g / 3.5 oz carrots
- 20 g / 0.7 oz gruyere
- 1 egg
- 50 g / 1.8 oz milk
- 1 knob of butter

Method:

1. Put the cubed carrots and cheese into the mixing bowl for 10 seconds, speed 4.
2. Stir the mixture with the spatula and add milk and eggs
3. Blend for 30 seconds, speed 8
4. Pour the mixture into a small buttered tin (18cm / 7 in diameter)
5. Cook in a preheated oven at 160° C / 320° F for about 10 minutes at 180°/ 360° F.

MEAT PIE

Ingredients:

- 100 g / 3.5 oz peeled potatoes
- 50 g / 1.8 oz rabbit or turkey
- 50 g / 1.8 oz milk
- 10 g / 0.4 oz parmesan
- 1 knob of butter.

Method:

1. With the blade in motion (speed 7), add the cubed potato and meat through the hole in the lid
2. Add the other ingredients for 30 seconds, speed 6
3. Stir the mixture with the spatula, add the milk and cook for 15 minutes at 90° C/195° F, speed 1
4. When cooked, add the parmesan for 40 seconds, speed 6
5. Pour the mixture into a small buttered tin (18 cm / 7 in diameter)
6. Cook in a preheated oven at 180° C/360° F for about 15 minutes.

POTATO PIE

Ingredients:

- 100 g / 3.5 oz peeled potatoes
- 10 g / 0.4 oz parmesan
- 1 egg
- 50 g / 1.8 oz milk

Method:

1. Put the parmesan into the mixing bowl for 10 seconds, speed 9
2. Add the cubed potatoes and egg for 30 seconds, speed 6
3. Add the milk for 20 seconds, speed 4
4. Pour the mixture into a small oiled and floured tin (18 cm / 7 in diameter)
5. Cook in a preheated oven at 200° C / 390° F for about 20 minutes

FISH GRATIN

Ingredients:

- 100 g / 3.5 oz peeled potato
- 70 g / 2.5 oz cod fillets
- 400 g / 14 oz water
- 10 g / 0.4 oz parmesan
- butter (to taste)
- a pinch of salt

Method:

1. Put the chopped potato and cod in the basket in the mixing bowl
2. Cook for 20 minutes at 100° C/ 210° F, speed
3. When cooked, remove the basket leaving 100 g / 3.5 oz cooking water in the mixing bowl.
4. Add the potato, cod, salt and half the parmesan for 40 seconds, speed 6
5. Pour the mixture into a small buttered tin (18 cm / 7 in diameter)
6. Sprinkle with the remaining parmesan and brown in a preheated oven at 180° C/ 360° F for 12 minutes.

SOLE WITH TOMATO

Ingredients:

- 100 g / 3.5 oz peeled potatoes
- 70 g / 2.5 oz sole fillets
- 1 ripe, deseeded tomato
- 300 g / 10.6 oz water
- 1 tablespoon extra virgin olive oil

Method:

1. Place the water and cubed potatoes in the mixing bowl for 20 minutes at 100° C/210° F, speed 1
2. Halfway through the cooking time, add the basket with the sole in and continue at speed 1
3. Remove the sole and drain the potatoes, retaining half a measure of cooking water
4. Add the tomato and salt and blend for 20 seconds, speed 6
5. Stir the mixture with the spatula and cook for 3 minutes at 90°-100° C/195°-210° F, speed 2

VEGETABLE TART

Ingredients:

- 1 peeled potato
- 1 peeled, deseeded tomato
- 1 zucchini
- 1 stick of celery
- 300 g / 10.6 oz water
- 100 g / 3.5 oz milk
- 1 pinch of salt

Method:

1. Put the water and cubed potatoes in the mixing bowl for 20 minutes at 100° C/210° F, speed 1
2. Drain the potato and put it back in the mixing bowl with the tomato, zucchini, celery, milk, salt and 15 g/ 0.4 oz of parmesan for 5 minutes at 90° C/195° F, speed 2
3. Pour the mixture into a small oiled, floured tin (18 cm/7 in diameter)
4. Sprinkle with the remaining parmesan and cook in a preheated oven at 180° C/360° F for 10 minutes

HAM SAUCE

Ingredients:

- 1 medium-sized ripe tomato, peeled
- 30 g / 1.1 oz cooked ham
- 1 teaspoon extra virgin olive oil
- a pinch of salt

Method:

1. Put the chopped tomato, ham and salt in the mixing bowl for 40 seconds, speed 6
2. Cook for 4 minutes at 90° C/195° F, speed 1
3. When cooked, add a teaspoon of oil

HAMBURGER WITH CHEESE

Ingredients:

- 40 g / 1.4 oz beef
- 30 g / 1.1 oz parmesan
- 300 g / 10.6 oz water
- a sprig of parsley
- 1 pinch of salt

Method:

1. With the blade in motion, insert the meat, parsley and parmesan through the hole in the lid and grind for 15 seconds
2. Shape the mixture into small hamburgers and arrange in the oiled basket
3. Add the water, position the basket and cook for 7 minutes at 100° C/210° F, speed 4 .
4. Remove the basket and arrange the hamburgers on the plate

Note: the leftover broth can be used to make a soup

HAM WITH SPINACH

Ingredients:

- 150 g / 5.3 oz spinach
- 1 peeled potato
- 40 g / 1.4 oz cooked ham
- 150 g / 5.3 oz milk
- a knob of butter
- a pinch of salt

Method:

1. Add the cubed potatoes and milk to the mixing bowl and cook for 5 minutes at 90° C/195° F, speed 1
2. Add the spinach through the hole in the lid for 5 minutes at 90° C/195° F, speed 1
3. Add the ham for 4 minutes at 90° C/195° F, speed 2 .
4. Stir the mixture with the spatula and blend for 40 seconds, speed 6
5. Add the butter and serve

STEAMED RICE

Ingredients:

- 40 g / 1.4 oz rice
- 400 g / 14 oz water
- 1 pinch of salt

Method:

- Add the water and salt to the mixing bowl and position the basket with the rice. Cook for 20 minutes at 100° C/210° F, speed 4

Note: when cooked, dress the rice with ham or tomato sauce, or with oil and parmesan.

VEGETABLE SOUP

Ingredients:

- 1\4 peeled potato
- 1\2 carrot
- 3 spinach leaves
- 1 piece of onion and celery
- 2 lettuce leaves
- 200 g / 7 oz water
- a pinch of salt
- 1 teaspoon of extra virgin olive oil

Method:

1. With the blade in motion (speed 6), insert the chopped vegetables through the hole in the lid
2. Stir the mixture with the spatula
3. Add the water and salt: cook for 12 minutes at 90°-100° C/195°-210° F, speed 2
4. Blend for 40 seconds, speed 6
5. Add oil and serve.

Note: The combined vegetables should weigh less than 100- 130 g/3.5-4.5 oz.

SCENTED TOMATO

Ingredients:

- 200 g / 7 oz ripe peeled, deseeded tomatoes
- 1 stick of celery
- 1 piece of carrot
- 1 sprig of parsley and basil
- 1 pinch of salt
- 1 teaspoon of extra virgin olive oil

Method:

1. Place the cubed vegetables in the mixing bowl for 20 seconds, speed 6
2. Season and cook for 12 minutes at 90° C/195° F, speed 2
3. Stir the mixture with the spatula and blend for 40 seconds, speed 6
4. Add oil and serve.

TOMATO SAUCE

Ingredients:

- 100 g / 3.5 oz ripe peeled, deseeded tomatoes
- 1 pinch of salt
- 1 teaspoon extra virgin olive oil

Method:

1. Put the tomato and salt in the mixing bowl for 20 seconds, speed 3
2. Cook for 5 minutes at 80° C/175° F, speed 1
3. Add the oil and finish cooking for a further 1 minute with the machine not in motion (if bitter, add a pinch of sugar)

FIRST BREAKFASTS

MILK AND RUSKS

Ingredients:

- 200 g / 7 oz milk
- 2 rusks
- 1 flat teaspoon of sugar

Method:

1. Place all the ingredients in the mixing bowl for 20 seconds, speed 5
2. Stir the mixture with the spatula and cook for 3 minutes at 70° C/160° F, speed 2
3. When cooked, blend for 20 seconds, speed 6
4. Pour into a cup and leave to cool.

COOKIE SMOOTHIE

Ingredients:

- 150 g / 5.3 oz fruit (apple and banana)
- 80 g / 2.8 oz milk
- 3 cookies
- a teaspoon of lemon juice

Method:

1. With the blade in motion, add the cookies to the mixing bowl, speed 4
2. crush for 30 seconds, speed 6
3. Add the chopped fruit, lemon juice and milk for 40 seconds, speed 9

BANANA SMOOTHIE

Ingredients:

- 120 g/ 4.2 oz milk
- 1 medium-sized ripe banana

Method:

1. With the blade in motion (speed 4), insert the banana through the hole in the lid
2. Add the milk for 30 seconds, speed 5
3. Stir the mixture with the spatula and cook for 3 minutes at 80° C/175° F, speed 2
4. When cooked, blend for 20 seconds, speed 6
5. Serve warm or cold.

RASPBERRY SMOOTHIE

Ingredients:

- 1 tablespoon of fresh raspberries
- 150 g / 5.3 oz milk

Method:

1. With the blade in motion (speed 4), insert the raspberries through the hole in the lid
2. Add the milk for 10 seconds, speed 5
3. Stir the mixture with the spatula and cook for 3 minutes at 80° C/175° F, speed 3
4. Serve warm or cold.

BANANA WITH VANILLA

Ingredients:

- 200 g / 7 oz milk
- 1 medium-sized ripe banana
- 1 vanilla pod

Method:

1. With the blade in motion (speed 6), insert the banana through the hole in the lid and continue for 10 seconds
2. Add the milk vanilla for 40 seconds, speed 6.
3. Serve cold or at room temperature.

ORANGE DRINK

Ingredients:

- 1 peeled, deseeded orange
- 100 g / 3.5 oz water
- 1 teaspoon of sugar or honey

Method:

1. Place the orange segments into the mixing bowl for 30 seconds, speed 4
2. Add the sugar and water for 40 seconds, speed 6
3. Serve immediately.

ENGLISH PORRIDGE

Ingredients:

- 1 measure of quick-cook rolled oats
- 300 g / 10.6 oz milk
- 1 teaspoon of sugar

Method:

1. Add the ingredients to the mixing bowl for 20 seconds at speed 6 and cook for 5 minutes at 90° C/195° F, speed 2
2. Leave to cool before serving.

FIRST ENGLISH BREAKFAST

Ingredients:

- 3 tablespoons of rice flakes
- 1 cookie
- 200 g / 7 oz milk

Method:

1. Place the ingredients in the mixing bowl for 20 seconds, speed 6
2. Cook for 3 minutes at 90° C/195° F, speed 2
3. Leave to cool before serving.

SMOOTHIE WITH RICE FLAKES

Ingredients:

- 30 g / 1.1 oz rice flakes
- 1 peeled peach
- 200 g / 7 oz milk

Method:

1. With the blade in motion (speed 4), add first the rice flakes, then the chopped peach through the hole in the lid
2. Add the milk and cook for 3 minutes at 100° C/210° F, speed 2
3. When cooked, stir the mixture with the spatula and blend for 40 seconds, speed 6
4. Serve warm or cold.

Note: You can replace the peach with apricot and the rice flakes with multi-grain flakes.

FRUIT JUICE

Ingredients:

- 3 ripe pears, peeled and deseeded (or apples, peaches or apricots)
- 2 tablespoons of sugar
- 250 g / 8.8 oz water
- a teaspoon of lemon juice

Method:

1. Add the water and sugar to the mixing bowl for 3 minutes at 90° C/195° F, speed 2
2. Add the fruit and lemon juice for 20 seconds, speed 6
3. Cook for 5 minutes at 90° C/195° F, speed 2
4. Blend for 40 seconds, speed 6
5. Serve warm or chilled.

24 MONTHS

FRESH PASTA SHAPES FOR BROTH

Ingredients:

- 1 egg
- 100 g /3.5 oz flour
- 20 g / 0.7 oz flour for kneading

Method:

1. Add the flour and egg to the mixing bowl and mix for 10 seconds, speed 5
2. With the blade in motion (speed 5), add the remaining 20 g / 0.7 oz flour and immediately stop the machine.
3. Remove the pasta dough and use immediately or leave to dry under a cloth.

PEA VELOUTÉ

Ingredients:

- 100 g / 03.5 oz peas
- 100 g / 3.5 oz (1 measure) of vegetable or meat broth
- 50 g / 1.8 oz (1/2 measure) of milk
- 1 teaspoon of extra virgin olive oil
- a pinch of salt

Method:

1. Put all the ingredients (except the oil) in the mixing bowl
2. Cook for 12 minutes at 90° c/195° F, speed 2
3. Stir the mixture with the spatula and blend for 40 minutes, speed 6.
4. When ready to serve, add 1 teaspoon of oil.

Note: the stated cooking time is for frozen peas.

BAKED CELERY

Ingredients:

- 100 g / 3.5 oz celery
- 100 g / 3.5 oz milk (1 measure)
- 30 g / 1.1 oz parmesan
- 1 tablespoon of flour
- 1 knob of butter
- 1 pinch of salt

Method:

1. With the blade in motion (speed 6), add the parmesan and celery through the hole in the lid
2. Add the milk, flour and salt and cook for 5 minutes at 80° C/175° F, speed 2
3. Pour the mixture into a buttered tin and brown in a preheated oven for 15 minutes at 170° C/340° F.

SPINACH TART

Ingredients:

- 150 g / 5.3 oz spinach, boiled and drained
- 60 g / 2.1 oz rabbit or turkey
- 100 g / 3.5 oz water
- 100 g / 3.5 oz milk
- 1 tablespoon of flour
- a pinch of salt

Method:

1. With the blade in motion (speed 6), add the meat through the hole in the lid
2. Add the spinach, flour, water, milk and salt and cook for 6 minutes at 90° C/195° F, speed 2
3. Pour the mixture into a small greased baking tray
4. Sprinkle with parmesan and brown in a preheated oven at 170° C/240° F for 15 minutes

STUFFED, BAKED ARTICHOKES

Ingredients:

- 1 whole artichoke, cooked
- 1/2 slice of lean cooked ham
- 20 g / 0.7 oz gruyere
- 1 hardboiled egg
- 50 g / 1.8 oz (1/2 measure) milk
- 1 sprig of parsley
- a pinch of salt

Method:

1. Remove the outer leaves of the artichoke and the hairy choke from the base. Keeping the artichoke whole, scoop out the flesh with a tablespoon
2. Put the artichoke flesh into the mixing bowl with the ham, gruyere, egg, milk, salt and parsley for 30 minutes, speed 6
3. Fill the base of the artichoke with stuffing
4. Bake in a preheated oven at 180° C/360° F for 13 minutes.

NOTE: The leftover stuffing can be used to make a soup by adding half a measure of milk and a pinch of salt and cooking for 5 minutes at 80° C/175° F, speed 2.

RAW SOUP

Ingredients:

- 350 g / 12.3 oz vegetable or meat broth
- 1/2 cooked potato
- 100 g / 3.5 oz mixed vegetables (celery, carrot, lettuce, zucchini, tomato)
- 1 teaspoon of extra virgin olive oil
- a pinch of salt

Method:

1. Put the broth in the mixing bowl for 6 minutes at 100° C/210° F, speed 1
2. Add the chopped vegetables for 20 minutes, speed 3 then for 40 minutes, speed 6.
3. Pour out and add the oil.

BOLOGNESE SAUCE

Ingredients:

- 30 g/ 1.1 oz meat
- 30 g / 1.1 oz celery
- 30 g / 1.1 oz carrots
- 100 g / 3.5 oz peeled tomatoes
- 1 teaspoon of extra virgin olive oil
- 1 pinch of salt

Method:

1. With the blade in motion (speed 7), add the meat through the hole in the lid
2. Add the carrot, celery, tomatoes and salt for 20 minutes, speed 6
3. Cook for 14 minutes at 90-100° C/195-210° F, speed 2.
4. When cooked, blend for 40 minutes, speed 6
5. Add the oil then serve.

STRAWBERRY CAKE

Ingredients:

- 100 g / 3.5 oz strawberries
- a tablespoon of flour
- 1 egg
- 150 g / 5.3 oz milk (1 measure and a half)
- 2 tablespoons of sugar
- 1 sachet of vanilla flavoring

Method:

1. Put the egg, flour, milk, sugar and vanilla in the mixing bowl for 15 minutes, speed 5
2. Cook for 3 minutes at 80° C/174° F, speed 4
3. Grease a small baking tray and spread out the chopped strawberries
4. Pour the mixture over the strawberries and cook in a preheated oven at 170° C/340° F for 15 minutes.

NOTE: If you wish, you can replace the strawberries with different fruit.

STRAWBERRY SNACK

Ingredients:

- 50 g / 1.8 oz strawberries
- 200 g / 7 oz milk
- 1 teaspoon of sugar

Method:

1. Put the strawberries and sugar in the mixing bowl for 30 minutes, speed 6
2. Add the milk and blend for 40 minutes, speed 6
3. Serve immediately.

COOKIE CAKE

Ingredients:

- 150 g / 5.3 oz dry cookies
- 20 g / 0.7 oz sugar
- 20 g / 0.7 oz barley coffee
- 1 egg
- 40 g / 1.4 oz butter

Method:

1. With the blade in motion (speed 4), add the cookies through the hole in the lid
2. Crush for 30 seconds at turbo speed and remove from the mixing bowl
3. Add the other ingredients for 20 seconds, speed 4
4. Stir the mixture with the spatula and cook for 3 minutes at 70° C/160° F, speed 2
5. Add the crushed cookies for 30 seconds, speed 5
6. Pour the mixture into one large mold or several small ones
7. Keep in the fridge for at least 24 hours
8. Serve with crème anglaise.

CREME ANGLAISE

Ingredients:

- 500 g / 17.6 oz milk (5 measures)
- 50 g / 1.8 oz sugar
- 1 egg
- 10 g / 0.4 oz cornflour
- 1 sachet of vanilla flavoring

Method:

1. Put all the ingredients in the mixing bowl for 10 seconds, speed 4
2. Cook for 10 minutes at 80° C/175° F, speed 4
3. Serve warm.

APPLE CAKE

Ingredients:

- 250 g / 8.8 oz peeled apples
- 70 g / 2.5 oz sugar
- 3 eggs
- 50 g / 1.8 oz (1 measure) flour
- juice of one lemon
- zest of half a lemon
- 1 knob of butter

Method:

1. Put 2 tablespoons of sugar in the mixing bowl for 40 minutes, turbo speed
2. Remove the sugar and put it aside
3. Put the remaining sugar in the mixing bowl with the lemon zest for 30 seconds, speed 6
4. Add the chopped apple, eggs, flour and lemon juice for 30 seconds, speed 6
5. Stir the mixture with the spatula and blend for 40 seconds, speed 6
6. Pour the mixture into an oiled, floured tray (20cm diameter)
7. Cook in a preheated oven at 180° C/360° F for 30 minutes

8. Leave to cook, remove from the tray and sprinkle with sugar before serving.

APPLE JAM

Ingredients:

- 500 g / 17.6 oz peeled, cored apples
- 200 g / 7 oz sugar
- the juice of one lemon

Method:

1. Put the chopped apple, sugar and lemon juice in the mixing bowl for 1 minute, turbo speed
2. Cook for 30 minutes at 100° C/210° F, speed 3
3. Pour into sterilized glass jars and boil for 10 minutes

NOTE: the jam can be kept for 2/3 weeks.

YELLOW MILK

Ingredients:

- 100 g / 3.5 oz milk (1 measure)
- 1 egg yolk
- one teaspoon of sugar

Method:

1. Put all the ingredients in the mixing bowl for 20 seconds, speed 6

CHOCOLATE DRINK

Ingredients:

- 200 g / 7 oz (2 measures) milk
- 2 teaspoons of bitter cocoa
- 1 teaspoon of sugar

Method:

- Put all the ingredients in the mixing bowl for 20 seconds, speed 6

NOTE: If you use sweetened cocoa, it is not necessary to add sugar.

PINEAPPLE ICE CREAM

Ingredients:

- 1 medium-sized pineapple, fresh and ripe
- 200 g / 7 oz sugar
- 100 g / 3.5 oz water (1 measure)
- the juice of 2 lemons

Method:

1. Put the water and sugar in the mixing bowl for 5 minutes at 90/100° C/195-210° F, speed 1.
2. Pour the syrup into a bowl and leave to cool
3. With the blade in motion (speed 6), add the chopped pineapple through the hole in the lid and continue for 20 seconds
4. Stir the mixture with the spatula, add the syrup and lemon juice for 20 seconds, speed 6
5. Pour into a large, shallow container and place in the freezer for 5/6 hours
6. When ready to serve, cut into wedges and place in the mixing bowl for 30 seconds, speed 8.

NOTE: You can replace the pineapple with other fruit.

EGG WHITE CAKE

Ingredients:

- 50 g / 1.8 oz flour
- 25 g / 0.9 oz sugar
- 20 g / 0.7 oz butter, softened
- 1 egg white
- 50 g / 1.8 oz milk
- 1 teaspoon baking powder

Method:

1. Position the butterfly whisk and whisk the egg white for 2 minutes at 40° C/100° F, speed 2-3
2. Remove the whisk and the egg white and (without rinsing the bowl) add the sugar, butter and milk for 40 seconds, speed 5
3. Stir the mixture with the spatula. Add the flour and baking powder for 30 seconds, speed 5
4. Add the whisked egg white to the mixture for 30 seconds, speed 2
5. Oil a 16 cm diameter tray, pour in the mixture and cook in a preheated oven for 20 minutes at 180° C/360° F.

If you wish you can add 2 teaspoons of cocoa.

MIXED FRUIT SORBET

Ingredients:

- 700 g / 24.7 oz peeled, frozen fruit (2 apples, 1 banana, 1 orange, 1 kiwi)
- 150 g / 5.3 oz sugar
- 2 peeled lemons

Method:

1. Put the sugar in the mixing bowl for 15 seconds, turbo speed
2. Add the chopped lemons for 15 seconds, turbo speed
3. Add the fruit. Stir, keeping the speed at 7 for 45 seconds

Seasonal fruit is recommended.

RING-SHAPED CAKE

Ingredients:

- 250 g / 8.8 oz flour
- 100 g / 3.5 oz sugar
- 1 egg
- 450 g / 15.9 oz milk
- 50 g / 1.8 oz butter
- yellow lemon zest
- 1 pinch of cinnamon
- 1 pinch of salt
- For the topping:
- 1 egg yolk
- 1 teaspoon of milk.

Method:

1. Bring the water to the boil in a large pan
2. With the blade in motion (speed 5), add the lemon zest through the hole in the lid for 20 seconds
3. Add the other ingredients for 20 seconds, speed 6

4. Remove the mixture from the mixing bowl and shape into a ring with a 4-5 cm diameter. Place in the boiling water.

5. When it rises to the surface, remove the ring and place on a buttered baking tray

6. Brush the cake with beaten egg and milk and cook in a preheated oven at 180° C/360° F for 30 minutes.

Boiling means the cake can be kept for several days. This step can be omitted if the cake is to be eaten immediately.

DAISY CAKE

Ingredients:

- 200 g / 7 oz sugar
- 6 eggs
- 125 g flour
- 125 g / 4.4 oz starch
- juice of 1/2 lemon
- 1 sachet of baking powder
- 1 sachet of vanilla flavoring
- 1 pinch of salt
- butter (to taste)

Method:

1. Put the sugar in the mixing bowl for 20 seconds, speed 9
2. Add the eggs for 20 seconds, speed 4
3. With the blade in motion (speed 5), add the flour, starch, salt, lemon juice and vanilla through the hole in the lid
4. Add the baking powder for 10 seconds, speed 4
5. Pour the mixture into a 24 cm diameter buttered, floured tray

6. Cook in a preheated oven at 160° C / 320° F for 10 minutes, then at 180° C/ 360° F for 15 minutes, and finally for 15 minutes at 200° C/390° F.

WHOLEMEAL DRINK

Ingredients:

- 1/2 lemon e 1/2 orange, peeled and deseeded
- 50 g / 1.8 oz sugar
- 150 g / 5.3 oz water

Method:

- Put the chopped fruit and sugar in the mixing bowl for 30 seconds at speed 3 and 30 seconds at speed 9
- Add the water for 40 seconds at speed 6
- Serve immediately

The same drink can be made by replacing the orange with other types of fruit.

SHORTCRUST PASTRY COOKIES

Ingredients:

- 300 g / 10.6 oz flour
- 50 g / 1.8 oz sugar
- 130 g / 4.6 oz butter
- 1 egg plus 2 yolks
- the zest of 1 lemon
- 1 pinch of salt

Method:

1. Put the lemon zest, sugar and 100 g /3.5 oz flour in the mixing bowl for 30 seconds, turbo speed
2. Add the remaining flour, eggs, butter and salt for 25 seconds, speed 3
3. Wrap the dough in greaseproof paper and leave to rest in the fridge for 10 minutes
4. On a floured surface, roll out the dough a a thickness of 1/2 cm and cut into the shapes of your choice
5. Arrange on an oiled baking tray lined with baking paper and cook in a preheated oven at 160° C/ 320° F for 15 minutes.
6. Remove from the tray when still warm.

GLUTEN-FREE RECIPES

PRECOOKED RICE FLOUR

Ingredients:

- 200 g / 7 oz rice

Method:

1. Put the rice in the mixing bowl and crush for 1 minute, turbo speed
2. Toast for 30 minutes at 100° C/ 210° F, speed 4.

Note: This method can be used for any type of cereal

GLUTEN-FREE PASTA SHAPES FOR BROTH

Ingredients:

- 250 g / 8.8 oz gluten-free flour
- 2 x 70 g / 2.5 oz eggs (if the eggs are smaller than this, add a little extra water)
- 20 g / 0.7 oz water
- 30 g / 1.1 oz extra virgin olive oil

Method:

1. Put all the ingredients in the mixing bowl for 30 seconds, speed 3
2. Remove the dough from the mixing bowl and divide into 4
3. With the blade in motion (speed 4), add the dough through the hole in the lid for 6/7 seconds before stopping the machine
4. Place the pasta on a cloth and repeat the process for the remaining quarters.

NOTE: If dried thoroughly, the pasta can be kept for several days.

DOUGH FOR GLUTEN-FREE BREAD

Ingredients:

- 350 g / 12.3 oz gluten-free flour
- 150 g / 5.3 oz water
- 150 g / 5.3 oz milk
- 1 sachet of gluten-free yeast (14 g/0.2 oz)
- 1 tablespoon extra virgin olive oil
- 1 pinch of sugar
- salt (to taste)

Method:

1. Put the water, milk and yeast in the mixing bowl for 2 minutes at 40° C/104° F, speed 3.
2. Add the flour, salt, sugar and oil for 30 seconds at speed 4, then 1 minute at spike speed
3. Using the spatula, remove the dough and leave to rise in a warm place for at least 1 hour
4. Once the dough has risen, flour your hands and shape the dough into small rolls
5. Arrange on a greased baking tray and leave to rise in a preheated oven at 30° C/85° F until it had doubled in volume
6. Remove the rolls from the oven and cover with a cloth. Preheat the oven to 200° C/390° F.

7. Cook for around 30 minutes.

DOUGH FOR GLUTEN-FREE PASTA

Ingredients:

- 200 g / 7 oz gluten-free flour
- 2 eggs
- 1 tablespoon of extra virgin olive oil
- salt (to taste)

Method:

1. Put all the ingredients in the mixing bowl for 30 seconds at speed 4, then 40 seconds at spike speed
2. Remove the dough, roll out and cut into shapes of your choice

NOTE: the firmness of the dough depends on the size of the eggs

GLUTEN-FREE APPLE CAKE

Ingredients:

- 4 measures gluten-free flour
- 3 pippin apples (400 g/ 14 oz)
- 100 g / 3.5 oz sugar
- 1 small vial of lemon essence

- 3 eggs
- 3 tablespoons of extra virgin olive oil
- 100 g / 3.5 oz milk
- 1 sachet of gluten-free yeast
- butter and sugar (to taste) to sprinkle on the cake

Method:

1. Position the butterfly whisk and put the sugar, lemon essence and eggs in the mixing bowl for 4 minutes, speed 2.
2. Without switching off the machine, with the blade in motion (speed 1) add the oil, milk, flour and yeast through the hole in the lid
3. Increase the speed to speed 2 and continue mixing for 8 minutes. Meanwhile, peel the apples and cut into slices.
4. Butter a 20/22 cm /8-8 ½ in diameter baking tray, pour in the mixture and arrange the apple slices in a sunburst pattern
5. Sprinkle with sugar and dabs of butter
6. Cook in a preheated oven at 180° C/360° F for about 40 minutes
7. Switch off the oven and leave the cake to rest inside for 5 minutes before removing.

GLUTEN-FREE CAMILLE

Ingredients:

- 250 g / 8.8 oz carrots
- 120 g / 4.2 oz sugar
- 100 g / 3.5 oz gluten-free flour
- 1 sachet of gluten-free yeast (10 g/0.4 oz)
- 50 g / 1.8 oz peeled almonds
- 2 small eggs
- lemon zest

Method:

1. Put the almonds, sugar and lemon zest in the mixing bowl for 20 seconds, turbo speed
2. With the blade in motion (speed 8), add the chopped carrots through the hole in the lid
3. Increase the speed to turbo for 25 seconds
4. Stir the mixture with the spatula and add the eggs for 5 seconds, speed 4.
5. Still with the blade in motion (speed 7), add the flour and yeast
6. Oil 6 paper cup cases, fill halfway with mixture and cook in a preheated oven at 180° C/360° F for about 30 minutes.

Note: The same recipe can be made substituting the gluten-free flour with 100 g /3.5 oz of starch and 50 g /1.8 oz cornflour, for a better result. However, the camille stay soft for several days.

GREEN APPLE MOUSSE

Ingredients:

- 3 green apples with peel
- 30 g / 1.1 oz potato starch
- 100 g / 3.5 oz sugar
- juice of one lemon.

Method:

1. Put all the ingredients in the mixing bowl for 30 seconds, speed 7.
2. Stir the mixture with the spatula and cook for 7 minutes at 90° C/195° F, speed 2
3. When cooked, blend for 40 seconds, speed 6
4. Pour into pots and rest in the fridge.

FRUIT JELLO

Ingredients:

- 300 g / 10.6 oz orange juice and juice of 1 lemon
- 200 g /7 oz peeled pippin apples
- 2 teaspoons of acacia honey
- 20 g / 0.7 oz leaf gelatin

Method:

1. Put the orange and lemon juice, chopped apple and honey in the mixing bowl for 30 seconds, speed 4
2. Cook for 5 minutes at 80° C/175° F, speed 2
3. Soften and drain the gelatin. Add for 2 minutes at 80° C/175° F, speed 3
4. When cooked, blend for 30 seconds, speed 6
5. Pour into a damp tray and leave to solidify in the fridge for at least 4 hours.

Thanks:

We thank the users of www.NoiMamme.it, especially Cristina Mazzaro for her work collecting and organizing the recipes presented here.

The proceeds of the ebook will go toward maintaining the NoiMamme.it site and community.

Publisher: RDC Network

Printed in Great Britain
by Amazon